JAPAN

This edition first published in 2011 in
the United States of America by
Marshall Cavendish Benchmark.

Marshall Cavendish Benchmark
99 White Plains Road
Tarrytown, NY 10591
Website: www.marshallcavendish.us

© Marshall Cavendish International (Asia)
Pte Ltd 2011
Originated and designed by Marshall Cavendish
International (Asia) Pte Ltd
A member of Times Publishing Limited
Times Centre, 1 New Industrial Road
Singapore 536196

Written by: Susan McKay
Edited by: Crystal Chan
Designed by: Lock Hong Liang
Picture research: Thomas Khoo

Library of Congress Cataloging-in-Publication Data
McKay, Susan, 1972-
Japan / by Susan McKay.
p. cm. -- (Festivals of the world)
Summary: "This book explores the exciting culture and
many festivals that are celebrated in Japan"--Provided
by publisher.
Includes index.
ISBN 978-1-60870-103-2
1. Festivals--Japan--Juvenile literature.
2. Japan--Social life and customs--
Juvenile literature. I. Title.
GT4884.A2M425 2011
394.26952--dc22
2009048275
ISBN 978-1-60870-103-2

Printed in Malaysia

1 3 6 5 4 2

Contents

4   Where's Japan?

6   What Are the Festivals?

8   Gion Festival

12   Children's Festivals

16 Fire Festivals

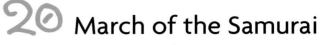
20 March of the Samurai

24 Snow Festival

26 Things for You to Do
  ✔ Make a Daruma Doll
  ✔ Make Onigiri

32 Glossary and Index

It's Festival Time . . .

The Japanese word for festival is *matsuri* [MAT-soo-ree]. There is a matsuri to celebrate everything from insects to wild horses. Many Japanese festivals are based on events in history. Others are based on religion or superstition. Whatever their origin, Japanese festivals are fun for all. Come make paper cranes, dress as a samurai, and build a snow statue. It's festival time in Japan!

Where's Japan?

Japan is a small group of islands lying between the Pacific Ocean and the Sea of Japan. There are four main islands in the **archipelago**: Hokkaido, Honshu, Kyushu, and Shikoku. Most people live on the main island, Honshu. The capital of Japan is Tokyo.

Who Are the Japanese?

A group of people called the **Ainu** [EYE-new] are believed to be the first settlers in what is now Japan. They are thought to have come to Japan from Siberia or possibly Australia. The other early settlers of Japan came mostly from China, Korea, Malaysia, and the South Pacific islands.

Over the centuries, the different groups began to fight, and eventually the Ainu settlers were driven to the northernmost island of Hokkaido. Today there are very few Ainu remaining, and their numbers are rapidly decreasing. The majority of Japanese are descendants of the migrants from China and Korea.

✳ A young Japanese boy dressed in traditional clothing.

CHINA

RUSSIA

SEA OF OKHOTSK

Hokkaido

Sapporo

N

NORTH KOREA

S E A   O F   J A P A N

Honshu

SOUTH KOREA

Mt. Fuji

TOKYO

Kyoto

Shimoda

Hiroshima

Yokohama

Fukuoka

Osaka

Nagasaki

Shikoku

Kyushu

E A S T   C H I N A   S E A

P A C I F I C   O C E A N

Okinawa

JAPAN

✳ Mount Fuji is the tallest mountain in Japan. On a clear day, people can see Mount Fuji from Tokyo, which is 75 miles (120 kilometers) away.

What Are the Festivals?

SPRING

* **Girl's Day**—Also referred to as the Doll Festival, this is a day to celebrate the health and happiness of young girls.

* **Buddha's Birthday**—Also known as *Hana Matsuri* or the Flower Festival, people celebrate the Buddha's birth by making offerings of fresh flowers at temples.

* **Setsubun**—A holiday in which people light lanterns and throw beans to chase away bad luck and to welcome good fortune for the spring.

* **Aoi Festival**—An imperial procession of people dressed in clothes from the Heian period (eighth–twelfth centuries).

* **March of the Samurai**—Commemorates a historical event that occurred in the year 1616.

* **Boy's Day**—A wind sock that resembles a carp is flown for each son in the family. In Japan, a carp is a symbol of strength and bravery.

* **Black Ship Festival**—This festival celebrates Commodore Perry's landing at Shimoda in 1854. On this day, there is a U.S. naval parade.

* **Peace Festival**—Japanese children make paper cranes and send them to Hiroshima to decorate the peace monument.

SUMMER

* **Gion Festival**—Celebrates Kyoto's triumph over disease many centuries ago. The main draw is a procession filled with elaborate floats.

* **Wild Horse Festival**—A Japanese horse race is held to honor the spirit of the samurai. People dress in traditional samurai uniforms from centuries ago.

* **Obon**—People welcome the spirits of their dead ancestors back into the home with huge feasts and special family celebrations.

* **Tanabata**—Bamboo cuttings are set up in houses and decorated with romantic poems to celebrate the legend of the weaver girl and the cowherd.

* **Daimonji Bonfire**—Huge bonfires are set ablaze to signal the end of summer and to symbolically light the way back to heaven for souls on the last day of their annual visit to earth.

AUTUMN

* **Shichi-Go-San**—A day for honoring children of the ages of three, five and seven, and praying for their welfare.

* **Roughhouse Festival**—Palanquins, carts lifted by people, are carried to the shrine where people perform for the gods and compete against other palanquin carriers.

* **Kurama Fire Festival**—Hundreds of bamboo torches are lit and carried to light the way for visiting deities.

* **Demon Dance**—Villagers present seven plays about hell.

WINTER

* **New Year**—The house is cleaned and decorated and temple bells are rung over one hundred times to mark the end of the old year and the beginning of the new one.

* **Nanakusa**—The seventh day of the New Year when all decorations are taken down and burned or thrown into the river as a form of purification.

* **Sapporo Snow Festival**—This festival features magnificent ice and snow sculptures and statues in the city of Sapporo, which gets a lot of snow in the winter.

* **Kamakura Festival**—People carve rooms out of snow mounds, and the historic Tsurugaoka Hachiman-gu shrine at the old capital city of Kamakura comes alive with age-old dance rituals and archery competitions.

* **Seijinshiki**—This is the day when young people celebrate turning twenty years old.

* **Namahage**—Adults dress up as monsters to scare children into being good in the coming year.

Get into the fighting spirit for the Roughhouse Festival!

7

Gion Festival

In mid-July, the city of Kyoto comes alive with hundreds of years of history. Kyoto is the ancient capital of Japan, so it is a special place for the Japanese. Thousands of people from across the country come to Kyoto and take to the streets to celebrate the Gion Festival.

✳ Every year, one boy is chosen to be the festival's page boy.

The Story of Gion

As the story goes, in the year 869, a terrible disease swept through the city of Kyoto. The emperor was concerned about his people, so he prayed to the gods for mercy. He went to Gion Shrine, which is now called the Yasaka Shrine, and made an offering of sixty-six halberds (spears with long handles and axe-like blades), one for each of his provinces. Soon after, the disease disappeared and the city was saved. The emperor was so pleased he organized a huge parade. The floats made for the parade were called *hoko* [HO-ko].

✳ Musicians surround the page boy at the top of the hoko.

What Are Hoko?

Hoko are huge floats that weigh as much as ten tons and measure as high as four stories. The hoko are so big and elaborate, they have to be put together about ten days before the festival. Each of the corners is supported by a giant wheel that is pulled forward by people walking on the ground. At the top of the float is a long pole that represents a halberd. The name of the hoko is determined by what is attached to the tip of the pole. If it is a half moon, for example, the hoko will be called the half moon-hoko.

The Page Boy

Every year, one lucky boy is chosen to be the festival's page boy. He dresses in the robe and hat of a priest, and he paints his face completely white. While the floats are being put together for the parade, the page boy walks around and keeps an eye on the progress. All day long he is followed by an attendant who holds an umbrella over his head to keep the hot sun off him. The boy's family also gets to join in the excitement by dressing up in special costumes.

✳ The night before the procession, paper lanterns are lit and strung throughout the city. The Yasaka Shrine below is the same shrine where the emperor prayed to the gods.

The Procession

When the day of the procession finally arrives, everyone is very excited. People travel from across Japan to be in Kyoto on this day. The people of Kyoto work very hard to put on the parade.

A priest purifies the hoko by pouring salt over the wheels. The page boy takes his place of honor in a seat at the top of the hoko. From there he can watch the procession and the people in the streets below him.

Young men dressed in short coats and straw hats are the crew of the hoko. When they get the signal, they start to pull on the long rope attached to the float. Slowly it begins to move. It will take many men to pull the hoko through the streets because it is so heavy, and the wooden wheels are hard to steer.

Older men dressed in ancient court costumes lead the march. More men climb on top of the hoko. Their sleeves are filled with *chimaki* [CHEE-ma-kee], straw or rice cakes wrapped in bamboo leaves. These are good luck charms. As the hoko makes its way through the streets, the men throw the charms to the crowd. Hundreds of people line the streets to watch the procession.

✳ This man is dressed in ancient court clothes for the Gion Festival.

✳ Opposite: Pulling the hoko is no easy job and requires many people working together.

This girl is resting after the long procession. When the sun goes down, she will light her lantern.

THINK ABOUT THIS

Kyoto is often called the "heart of old Japan" because it was the home of the imperial court for more than one thousand years. You can still see palaces in Kyoto today. Can you think of any other countries that have moved their capital from one city to another?

Ready for Next Year

By the end of the day, the hoko crew are very tired. Boys from the crowd rush toward the hoko so they can help pull, too. The procession ends when the hoko finally reaches its starting point. After a rest, each hoko is taken apart and stored away until next year. The panels must be handled with great care because many of them are hundreds of years old. They are considered works of art because of their intricate patterns and designs.

Children's Festivals

It is wonderful to be a child in Japan because there are many holidays to celebrate childhood. There are special days for girls, boys, and for children of different ages. Usually, Japanese children wear Western clothes, but during children's festivals, they dress in their best **kimono** [kee-MO-no], a long robe with wide sleeves.

Shichi-Go-San

Shichi-Go-San falls on November 15. The name of the festival literally means seven-five-three. It is called Shichi-Go-San because the festival honors children of those ages. On this day, parents give thanks for their children's health and wellness.

The day usually begins with a visit to the shrine. Parents pray to the gods to give their children health and happiness. Vendors outside the shrine sell candy wrapped in a long, brightly colored bag. The candy is said to bring good luck and a long life to those who eat it. Children have parties and also receive presents on this day.

✳ Boys wear kimonos, too. Only they wear theirs with wide, pleated pants called **hakama** [HA-ka-ma].

✳ Opposite: This seven-year-old is dressed in her best kimono for Shichi-Go-San.

Boy's Day

This day is also known as the Iris Festival or Children's Day, but it really belongs to boys. On the morning of May 5, the whole family takes a special bath, called *Shobu-ya*. The bath is said to wash away any bad luck. If iris leaves, *shobu* [SHO-boo] in Japanese, are put in the bath water, the boy will become strong and brave.

✳ Carp wind socks blow in the sky. Carp must fight their way upstream to lay their eggs. This is why they represent strength.

In front of the house, there is another symbol of strength and courage—the carp. A few days before May 5, cloth carp are hung from bamboo poles. The wind socks are flown throughout the holiday. There is a carp for each son. The largest fish at the top of the pole is for the eldest son. The smaller ones below are for the younger sons.

Folktales and Warriors

In nearly every Japanese home, there is a small area where scrolls hang to mark a special holiday. To honor boys, families decorate the area with toy weapons and famous warriors wearing traditional armor. Many of the warriors are well-known figures in Japanese history or folktales, such as Kintaro, the Golden Boy, and Momotaro, the Peach Boy, who battled against the wicked giants.

✳ Many Japanese boys hope to grow up as strong and brave as warriors.

Girl's Day

When March comes around, there is an air of excitement in families with daughters. Small boxes that have been stored all year are opened again. Inside them are dolls called **hina** [HEE-na]. The set of dolls is a special collection gathered by the family over many years. The set includes a prince, a princess, ladies-in-waiting, a minister of state, court musicians, and courtiers.

How Did the Festival Begin?

In the past, Girl's Day marked the beginning of spring. In those days, people rubbed themselves with paper dolls to get rid of winter. Then they threw the dolls into the river to be carried away. Over time, sculptors began to make clay dolls. The dolls were so beautiful that no one wanted to throw them away. Soon the tiny figures were kept year after year as a set. Today girls are told that March 3 is a lucky day to get married.

✳ These two young girls are all set for their Girl's Day celebration.

Fire Festivals

In the past, Japanese houses were made of wood and paper. Fire was both feared and respected because one tiny spark could set a whole village ablaze and leave thousands homeless.

✳ The master of ceremonies takes his seat at the fire festival.

According to the Japanese religion Shinto, fire is purifying and can protect people from bad spirits. Fire is honored by the Japanese at the many fire festivals that take place throughout the country.

These brave Shinto priests walk over hot coals.

Opposite: Men set the coals on fire.

Fire Walking

Every year in August and September, Shinto priests and followers take part in a fire-walking ceremony. Branches of firewood are bundled together and used to set a bed of coals on fire. The priests walk around the coal beds until they are in a trancelike, or extremely relaxed, state. Then they throw a handful of salt onto the coals, rub salt on the bottoms of their feet, and walk slowly and calmly over the burning hot coals.

The reason the priests perform this ceremony every year is to prove to people that fire can be controlled. Throughout the ceremony, the priests chant prayers, which are believed to help them conquer the fire.

Each year Mount Wakakusayama is the site of a grass-burning ceremony. This is to commemorate the friendly rivalry between two temples. The day ends with a huge fireworks display.

Kurama Fire Festival

In the village of Kurama, another fire festival takes place every year. The highlight is a procession led by children. Adults wearing short cotton coats follow behind them. All the marchers hold flaming torches or baskets of branches high up in the air. The flames begin to grow higher and sparks fly through the air. The fire is believed to protect people from bad spirits.

✳ Some risk takers try to catch the sparks because they believe they will bring them good luck.

The Fire Gods

Bonfires line the main street of the tiny village. The parade goes up and down the street until the younger torchbearers grow tired. Shortly before midnight, the crowd gathers and heads toward the village shrine. When they have reached the shrine, the Shinto priest whispers a farewell prayer to the fire gods to leave the village until next year.

March of the Samurai

There is a saying in Japan that goes "Never say *kekko* [KE-ko] until you have seen Nikko." The word *kekko* means magnificent, and Nikko is the beautiful town where the March of the Samurai takes place every year on May 17 and 18.

The Shogun's Shrine

The tradition of the March of the Samurai can be traced back to a very old story. In the twelfth century, a military dictator, called **shogun** (SHO-goon], ruled Japan. The shogun kept his power through his special army of warriors called samurai.

Many years later, in 1616, a very powerful shogun died. His grandson decided to build an elaborate shrine decorated with carvings and sheets of gold in his honor. On the day that his body was moved to the shrine, there was a huge procession of all the samurai in the shogun's army.

Every year, the March of the Samurai recreates the scene that first took place in 1616.

✳ Shinto priests play an important role in the festival.

The Procession

A Shinto priest on horseback leads the procession through the streets to the shrine. Behind him come the townspeople, wearing the dress of storekeepers, artists, performers, and warriors from hundreds of years ago. Musicians march along with the procession, providing entertainment.

One group of strong, young men is in charge of carrying a large metal box called a **palanquin**. It is said to hold the spirit of the shogun who died in 1616. Although his body is still buried in the shrine, some people pretend that he is being carried to his resting place, just as he was hundreds of years ago.

* Shinto priests walk in the March of the Samurai.

* It takes many strong people to lift the palanquin because it is very heavy.

Samurai

The samurai of Japan were a lot like the knights of medieval Europe. They were great warriors who were not afraid to fight and die for their ruler. Samurai always carried two swords. They were very experienced in fencing, wrestling, archery, and horsemanship. In battle, they wore unusually shaped helmets and heavy armor made of metal strips held together with leather and cords.

During the procession, people dress as samurai from the seventeenth and eighteenth centuries. Some carry only a bow and arrow. Others carry swords and spears. Still others carry matchlock guns that were introduced to Japan by the Portuguese in the sixteenth century.

❋ Men taking part in the March of the Samurai procession wear their full-battle costumes.

THINK ABOUT THIS
The name of the shogun who is commemorated in Nikko each year is Tokugawa Ieyasu. Today he is considered one of the greatest and bravest warriors of all time.

✳ Children also get to take part in the procession.

Yabusame

There is an exciting contest to end the day. It is a competition that tests the skill of archers on horseback. It is called **yabusame** [ya-boo-SA-may], and it was one of the favorite sports of the samurai.

Six small, square targets are attached to a fence that surrounds the playing ground. The rider has to race down the course toward the first three targets at a full gallop and try to hit these targets as he passes them. Then he must quickly turn around and ride back the other way to hit the three targets at the other end. It takes a bowman with great skill to hit all six targets in one try!

✳ Archers carry special bows and arrows to compete in yabusame.

Snow Festival

In most of Japan, there is not much snow in winter. However, in the northern city of Sapporo, there is heavy snowfall. That's why every year, on the second Thursday of February, the Sapporo Snow Festival is held. The city's main square becomes a showcase for ice sculptures and snow statues, some of them over 60 feet (18 meters) high.

Getting Ready for the Fun

The city prepares for the festival two weeks in advance. Trucks dump huge loads of snow in the main square. Big blocks of ice are taken from the frozen river. A team of sculptors is assigned one area to work in. They use tools to carve the ice and snow just as if it were marble.

* After two weeks, everything is ready for opening night. On this night, ice-skating and skiing contests are held. Most people come to enjoy the beautiful sculptures under a bright, colorful display of fireworks.

Things for You to Do

Spring is a special time in Japan because it is cherry blossom season. Cherry blossoms begin to bloom in February on the southern island of Okinawa. During the next few months, they blossom all across the country, finally opening on the northern island, Hokkaido, in May. The blossoms only last for about a week, so Japanese people gather in parks to celebrate the sight while it lasts. Here is a great activity and a special song to honor the cherry blossom festival.

Origami Blossoms

Making *origami* [o-ree-GA-mee] blossoms is easy. You will need several 5-inch (12.5-cm) squares of pink and white tissue paper and a few 3-inch (7.5-cm) pieces of green wire.

Stack a few sheets of paper and fold them in half diagonally. Unfold the paper and refold it into a rectangle. Fold it once more in half to make a square. Then unfold the paper completely.

Place the two diagonal corners together, and press in the sides along the creases. You should be holding a square now. Fold the square in half to make a triangle. Now make a hook at one end of the wire and staple it to the corner of the folded paper. Cut the top of the paper into a semicircle and make a fringe. Carefully pull back each layer of paper. Now position the layers to make the paper flower look like a real one.

CHERRY BLOSSOMS

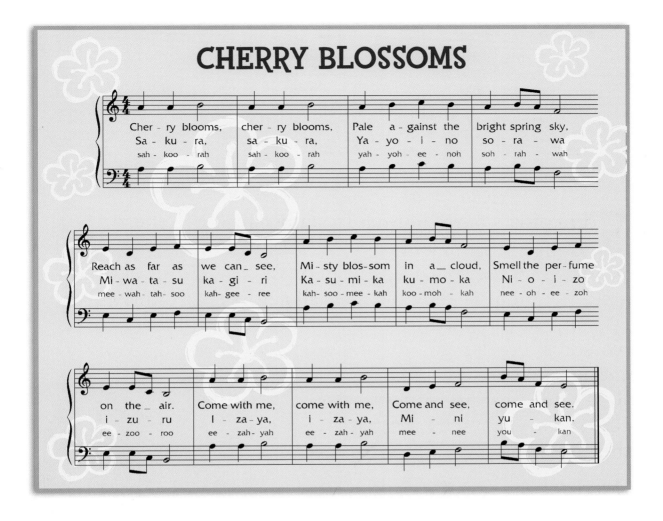

FURTHER INFORMATION

Books: *Girls' Day/Boys' Day.* Minako Ishii (Bess Press, 2007).

Japanese Celebrations: Cherry Blossoms, Lanterns and Stars! Betty Reynolds (Tuttle Publishing, 2006).

Life in Ancient Japan. Hazel Richardson (Crabtree Publishing Company, 2005).

Websites: www.jnto.go.jp/eng/indepth/history/index.html—Includes detailed sections on Japan's traditional annual events, food, culture, and history.

web-japan.org/atlas/index.html—A visual and informative tour across several topics, from historic sites and traditional crafts, to architecture and nature.

Make a Daruma Doll

The most common time to see a *daruma* [da-ROO-ma] doll is in late December. When they are sold, the dolls don't have eyes. That's because one eye is drawn in on New Year's Day when a wish is made. The other eye isn't drawn in until the wish comes true.

You will need:
1. Old newspapers
2. Flour-and-water paste
3. A balloon
4. Scissors
5. Paints
6. Paintbrushes
7. A pencil or pen
8. A paint tray
9. Masking tape
10. Glue
11. Cardboard

1 Blow up a round balloon until it is slightly smaller than your head. Using strips of newspaper and a flour-and-water paste, papier-mâché the balloon until it is completely covered. Allow it to dry.

2 For the base, cut a 2-inch (5-cm) strip from the cardboard. Make small cuts in the strip. Attach the two ends with masking tape. Turn in the cut sections. Glue the strip to the bottom of the balloon.

3 Using a pencil or pen, draw the face of the doll on the surface of the balloon.

4 Now paint the doll using bright, festive colors, such as red and gold. Be sure not to paint in the eyes yet!

Make Onigiri

A favorite Japanese snack at festival time is ***onigiri*** [o-NEE-gee-ree]. These delicious and healthy snacks are made from rice. Sometimes the rice is wrapped in seaweed. Other times it is covered with sesame seeds. You can put whatever you like inside, or follow this recipe and use sour plums, which you can find at an Asian market.

You will need:
1. 1 cup (225 g) rice
2. 1 1/4 cups (300 ml) water
3. 3 sour plums
4. 1 sheet dried seaweed
5. Salt
6. A cutting board
7. A saucepan
8. A wooden spoon
9. A measuring cup
10. A knife and an adult helper
11. Scissors
12. A plate
13. 1/4 cup (40 g) roasted sesame seeds

1 With an adult's help, put the rice in a saucepan with 1 1/4 cups water. Bring the water to a boil on high heat and cover the pan. Lower the heat when you see steam coming from the edge of the lid. Simmer rice for 12–13 minutes on low heat.

2 While the rice is cooking, ask your adult helper to make a slit in the plums with a knife and remove the pit from inside.

3 After the rice has cooled completely, pick up a handful and make a well in the middle. Put a sour plum inside, then put some salt in your hands. Then squeeze the rice to make a triangle. Be sure to close up the middle completely so the plum is not showing. Repeat this step with the other two plums.

4 Ask your adult helper to cut the seaweed into strips. Now wrap the rice triangle in seaweed or coat with sesame seeds. Onigiri is eaten hot or cold with your fingers.

Glossary

Ainu	The early settlers of Japan.
archipelago	A group of islands.
chimaki	Lucky charms made from straw or rice cakes wrapped in bamboo leaves.
daruma	A New Year's doll said to make wishes come true.
hakama	Formal dress for males.
hina	A special set of dolls collected for Girl's Day.
hoko	The Japanese word for halberd. Floats made for the Gion Festival.
kimono	Traditional Japanese dress.
onigiri	Snacks made from rice and seaweed or sesame seeds.
origami	Japanese paper folding.
palanquin	A box supported by poles and carried on the shoulders.
shogun	A military leader in twelfth to nineteenth century Japan.
yabusame	A contest that tests the skill of archers on horseback.

Index

Ainu, 4
Aoi Festival, 6

Black Ship Festival, 6
Boy's Day, 6, 14
Buddha's Birthday, 6

cherry blossoms, 26–27
children's festivals, 12–15

Daimonji Bonfire, 6
daruma, 28
Demon Dance, 7
dolls, 15, 28–29

fire festivals, 16–19
fire walking, 16–17

Gion Festival, 6, 8–11
Girl's Day, 6, 15

Hiroshima, 6

Japan, map of, 5

Kamakura Festival, 7
Kurama Fire Festival, 7, 18–19
Kyoto, 8, 10, 11

March of the Samurai, 20–23
Mount Fuji, 5
Mount Wakakusayama, 18

Namahage, 7
Nanakusa, 7
New Year, 7
Nikko, 20, 23

Obon, 6
onigiri, 30–31

Peace Festival, 6

Roughhouse Festival, 7

samurai, 6, 20, 22, 23
Seijinshiki, 7
Setsubun, 6
Snow Festival, 7, 24–25

Shichi-Go-San, 7, 12–13
Shinto, 16, 17, 19, 20, 21

Tanabata, 6
Tokugawa Ieyasu, 23
Tokyo, 4, 5

Wild Horse Festival, 6

yabusame, 23

Photo Credits
Alamy/Photolibrary: cover, 1, 3 (top), 5, 19 (bottom), 20; BES Stock: 2, 8 (bottom), 12, 14 (top and bottom), 15, 18, 23 (bottom), 25; Getty Images: 7 (bottom), 17, 21 (bottom); Haga Library: 6, 19 (top); Hutchison Library: 9, 10, 11 (top), 23 (top); Image Bank: 3 (bottom), 4, 7 (top); Japan National Tourist Organization: 26, 28; PANA: 24; Photolibrary: 13, 16 (both), 21 (top), 22; 22; Richard l'Anson: 8 (top), 11 (bottom)